eyew👁nder
Oceans

THIRD EDITION
Senior Editor Rupa Rao
Project Art Editor Revati Anand
US Senior Editor Shannon Beatty
US Executive Editor Lori Cates Hand
Picture Researcher Shubhdeep Kaur
Deputy Manager, Picture Research Virien Chopra
Managing Editors Gemma Farr, Kingshuk Ghoshal
Managing Art Editors Govind Mittal, Elle Ward
DTP Designer Vikram Singh
Production Editor Vishal Bhatia
Production Controller Joss Moore
Jacket Designer Vidushi Chaudhry
DK Delhi Creative Head Malavika Talukder
Art Director Mabel Chan
Managing Director Sarah Larter

Consultant Helen Scales

FIRST EDITION
Written and edited by Samantha Grey
Publishing Manager Mary Ling
Picture Researcher Nicole Kaczynski
Consultant Sue Thornton
With thanks to Sarah Walker for editorial assistance.

This American edition, 2025
First American Edition, 2003
Published in the United States by DK Publishing,
a division of Penguin Random House LLC
1745 Broadway, 20th Floor, New York, NY 10019

Published in Great Britain by Dorling Kindersley Limited
A catalog record for this book is available from the
Library of Congress.
ISBN 978-0-5939-6751-5

DK books are available at special discounts when
for sales promotions, premiums, fund-raising, or educational use.
For details, contact: DK Publishing Special Markets,
1745 Broadway, 20th Floor, New York, NY 10019
SpecialSales@dk.com

Printed and bound in China

www.dk.com

MIX
Paper | Supporting
responsible forestry
FSC™ C018179

This book was made with Forest
Stewardship Council™ certified
paper—one small step in DK's
commitment to a sustainable future.
**Learn more at www.dk.com/uk/
information/sustainability**

Contents

Ocean zones

Oceans may be divided into five zones according to how far down sunlight reaches. Different creatures live in one or more zones, having adapted to surviving at those depths.

Key

In this book, you will meet creatures that live in different ocean zones. You can use this key to tell you where each kind can be found.

Sunlit zone
0–660 ft (0–200 m)

Twilight zone
660 ft–3,300 ft (200 m–1,000 m)

Midnight zone
3,300 ft–13,200 ft (1,000 m–4,000 m)

Abyss
13,200 ft–19,700 ft (4,000 m–6,000 m)

Trenches
19,700 ft–36,000 ft (6,000 m–11,000 m)

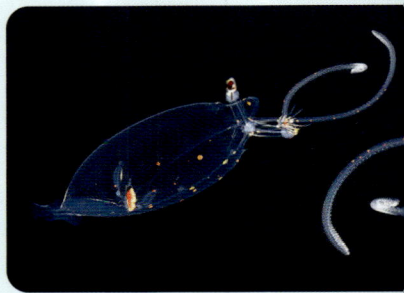

 ## HYDROTHERMAL VENTS

Hydrothermal vents, also known as black smokers, are hot springs pouring from rocky chimneys on the deep seabed. Even though they are hot and full of toxic chemicals, they are home to many creatures of the deep, ranging from tiny bacteria to tubeworms and fish.

Sunlit zone

Sunlight reaches down to about 660 ft (200 m) deep. Most sea creatures live in sunlit water. Sunlight reaches through shallow seas and the upper waters of the open ocean.

Twilight zone

Light becomes dim below 660 ft (200 m). The twilight zone extends to about 3,300 ft (1,000 m) below sea level. Creatures that live here include the glass squid. Its transparent body hides it from predators.

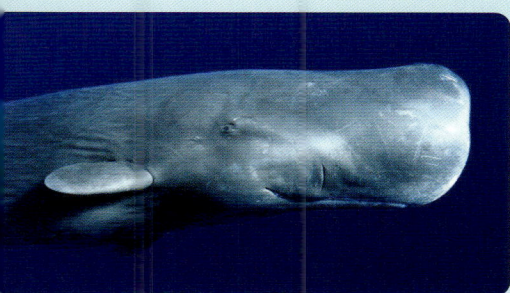

Midnight zone

No sunlight reaches below 3,300 ft (1,000 m) under the ocean, so the midnight zone is pitch black and extremely cold. Sperm whales dive into this zone to chase after squid.

Abyss

The dark region called the abyss starts from about 13,200 ft (4,000 m) down to around 19,700 ft (6,000 m). Creatures that are able to survive on the deep seabed or ocean floor include the sea cucumber.

Trenches

Ocean trenches are deeper than 19,700 ft (6,000 m). Here, the seabed or ocean floor can be about 36,000 ft (11,000 m) underwater. Animals living in trenches, such as this snail fish, are able to survive the huge water pressure.

The blue planet

Oceans cover more than two-thirds of Earth's surface. This vast underwater world is home to many creatures, often hidden beneath the waves.

Long, stiff wings help the bird glide over open waters.

Manx shearwater

Fishing for food

Seas and oceans are a source of food for many seabirds. Shearwaters spend most of their life out at sea.

One big ocean

If you traveled in a boat, you could sail to every ocean and almost every sea because they all join up in a big body of water.

 BLOWHOLE BREATHING

Whales are mammals. Unlike fish, they cannot breathe underwater. They surface to breathe air through their blowholes. A whale must surface every hour or so. Here, a southern right whale surfaces in the waters of the Indian Ocean near the Australian coast.

The Pacific Ocean covers more than a third of Earth's surface.

Plankton

The sunlit ocean teems with tiny life forms called plankton. They are a vital food source for many sea creatures.

Earth looks blue from outer space because water covers so much of its surface.

The plankton are so small that you need a microscope to see most of them.

Fast facts

The largest areas of seawater are called oceans. The smaller ones are called seas.

All seawater is salty. One of the saltiest seas is the Dead Sea.

From base to peak, the tallest mountain on Earth is Mauna Kea in Hawaii, but most of it sits under the Pacific Ocean.

Green turtles develop a greenish color from eating seagrasses and algae.

Sea turtles

There are many types of sea creature, including reptiles such as turtles. They have to rise to the surface for air. They breathe air through their nostrils.

What is a fish?

Vertebrates are animals with a backbone. A fish is a vertebrate that lives in water. All fish have gills for breathing underwater and fins for swimming. Most are covered in scales like tiles on a roof.

The lateral line on a fish senses ripples in the water and helps it find food.

Overlapping scales

Many fish have excellent eyesight.

Orange basslet

Pectoral fin

Opening to gills

How fish breathe

On land, oxygen is in the air. Water also contains oxygen. Fish gulp water and run it over their gills. Oxygen passes across the gills into the fish's blood.

Super senses

Fish have taste buds in their mouths, fins, and skin. They can also hear and smell. The great white shark (left) can smell a drop of blood from 0.25 miles (0.4 km) away.

SWIM LIKE A FISH!

Most fish swim like snakes wriggle. Their bodies form S-shaped curves. Usually, fish use their tails for the main push forward. A few row themselves along with their pectoral fins.

Catsharks wiggle from side to side.

Small-spotted catshark

Safety in schools

Small fish such as saupe often swim in large groups called schools, or shoals. There is safety in numbers!

Many fish are teardrop-shaped, which helps them glide swiftly through the water.

Dragon of the sea

Leafy sea dragons live in shallow, seaweedy waters. Here, they avoid predators by looking like seaweed.

Stonefish change color to look like part of the seabed. They have spines on their backs that inject venom if touched. This is one of the most venomous fish in the world.

Lionfish can spread their fins like a peacock spreads its feathers.

Prickly beauty

Lionfish have striped bodies to warn away other fish. Any predator that tries to bite a lionfish might be pierced by venomous spines.

Fantastic fish

Weird and wonderful fish vary in size from tiny sea horses to giant rays. Some have unusual shapes that help them hide or scare off predators.

A puffed-up porcupine fish has raised spines.

Puffed up

When in danger, porcupine fish gulp down water and swell up like balloons. Now they are too large and prickly for most predators to swallow.

A relaxed porcupine fish, with its spines lying flat

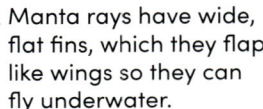

Manta rays have wide, flat fins, which they flap like wings so they can fly underwater.

Gentle giants

Manta rays are huge. They mainly eat plankton, which they gulp with their enormous mouths and filter out with parts of their gills called rakers.

Colorful ribbon

Ribbon eels can coil themselves into crevices that seem too small for their long bodies. They have sharp teeth for seizing prey.

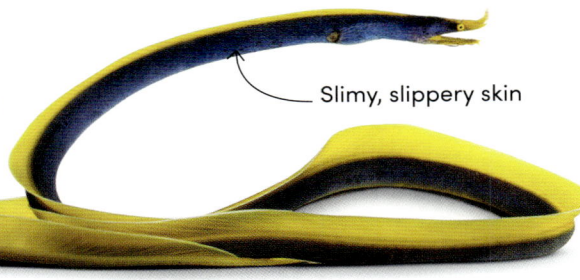

Slimy, slippery skin

Jellyfish

Ocean-living jellyfish are more than 95 percent water. They have no brains, bones, or hearts. Their stinging tentacles act like fishing lines to catch prey.

A jellyfish can get around by moving its soft body in and out like an umbrella.

Some jellyfish have short, stout tentacles.

Dinner delivered

Long tentacles trail from the jellyfish's body. When a small animal swims into the tentacles, they spear it with venomous stings.

Stinger

What's that word?

Invertebrate Despite their name, jellyfish are not fish. They are invertebrates. An invertebrate is an animal without a backbone.

Transparent A transparent animal or object is one that can be seen through.

Jellyfish may look like parachutes but they are probably traveling upward!

Up, up, and away

Some jellyfish are attracted to light and can be found near the water's surface. But many live in the deep sea during the day and then swim upward to the surface at night. This may keep them safe from predators.

Jellyfish have special cells that produce light.

Ghostly glow

Many jellyfish are nearly transparent. Some also produce their own light, so that they glow in dark water. They may only do this when disturbed.

OCEAN DRIFTER

In warmer parts of the world, the Portuguese man-of-war drifts on the surface of the waves. It is held up by a balloon-like float. This relative of jellyfish catches fish in its long tentacles. These shoot tiny stings into any animal that touches them.

Spectacular sharks

 Sharks are survivors! They have lived in the oceans since prehistoric times. They have powerful bodies, good hearing, and a keen sense of smell for sniffing out food.

A shark's dorsal fin helps it to swim in a straight line.

Sleek shark

A strong swimmer, the sandbar shark slices through the ocean at speed. It swims vast distances to find food.

Powerful predator

Great whites are the largest carnivorous fish. Some people think of them as ferocious hunters that attack humans. But, in fact, they do not attack humans unless they accidentally mistake a surfer for a seal!

Underwater leopards

Leopard sharks are named for their golden, spotted skin. This is good camouflage on the seabed where they search for their favorite food—clams.

Hammer-like head

Flat-faced shark

Hammerhead sharks have eyes at each end of their unusual, flat heads. This allows them to see in all directions at once!

If a great white bites a human, it usually spits them out.

👁 **LARGEST FISH**

Larger than every other type of shark is the whale shark—the biggest fish in the sea today! Whale sharks are gentle giants, with about 3,000 tiny teeth that are too small for a bite. They spend their time filtering tiny plankton.

Swimming lesson

A baby whale is called a calf. Young calves, such as this sperm whale calf, swim close to their mothers. It takes time for a calf to become a strong swimmer.

The head of a sperm whale can be up to 20 ft (6 m) long—larger than that of any other mammal.

The big blue

The blue whale is larger than any other animal on our planet. It can grow up to a staggering 100 ft (30 m) in length. Five humans could fit into the chambers of its massive heart!

👁 BALEEN OR TEETH?

When feeding, a baleen whale, such as a humpback, gulps water and strains it out through the baleen plates in its mouth. This traps tiny animals for it to eat. A toothed whale, such as an orca, has small, sharp teeth to grab fish and other prey.

Baleen plates

Teeth

Humpback whale

Orca

Leaping out of the water is called breaching.

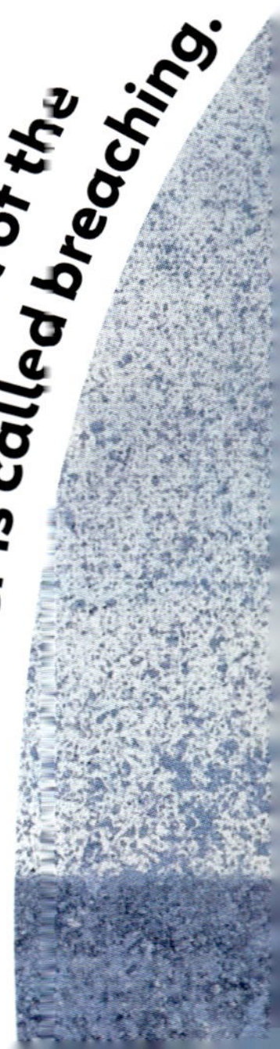

Ocean giants

Whales are the largest creatures in the ocean. Like all mammals, they breathe air. Whales take in air through openings called blowholes on their heads. There are two types of whale—baleen whales and toothed whales.

Splashing around

Humpback whales have longer flippers than other whales. They slap their flippers on the water to make loud splashes. This is called flippering!

Friendly creatures

Intelligent and curious, dolphins can be friendly toward people. They have even rescued shipwreck survivors and helped them back to shore!

Peas in a pod

Using a language of clicks and squeaks, pods of dolphins find their way around the ocean. They organize fish hunts by sending messages to each other. To stun fish, they may make very loud noises!

Flexible, muscular tail to zip through the water at great speed

Playful dolphins

Dolphins are small, toothed whales. These speedy swimmers race along with long, low leaps. Their streamlined body helps them glide through water easily.

Antarctic creatures

Hourglass dolphins live in the icy seas around Antarctica. They are the world's most southerly dolphins.

Dolphins often stroke each other with their flippers to make friends.

The long snout is called a beak.

Fast facts

Dolphins live in groups called pods. These may join together to form a superpod.

There are dolphins in all the world's oceans.

If a dolphin is sick or injured, other dolphins may support it with their bodies so that its blowhole is above the water's surface.

Gentle sea cows

Manatees and dugongs are large mammals that live in warm, shallow waters. They swim slowly, grazing on seagrass, so they are also called "sea cows."

FUNNY FACE

Like manatees, the dugong has no front teeth! Its teeth grow only along the sides of its mouth. Flippers steer and scoop up food.

Dugongs often dig down into the sand to eat seagrass roots.

Dugongs and manatees have few natural enemies.

Noises in the night

Dugongs feed during the day and night. Like manatees, they are noisy eaters. There are loud sounds of chomping teeth and flapping lips!

What's the difference?

Dugongs have a pointy, forked tail, while manatees have a paddle-shaped tail. They are the only plant-eating sea mammals.

A dugong has a forked tail like a dolphin.

Manatees sometimes have algae growing on their backs.

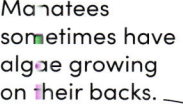

Motherly love

Dugongs and manatees give birth to only one calf every three to five years. The newborn calf rises to the surface immediately for its first breath of air.

Fast facts

Dugongs and manatees are related to elephants.

On meeting, sea cows grab each other's flippers, and then put their mouths together as if to kiss.

Manatees and dugongs can live for as long as 60 years.

The manatee's tail is flat like a paddle.

Soaring seabirds

Some seabirds live along the shore. Others fly far out to sea. All return to the shore to nest. Many nest in groups called colonies. They often choose cliffs where eggs and chicks are safe from predators.

Gannets can hold their breath under water for up to 40 seconds.

👁 LONG DISTANCES

The small Arctic tern flies longer distances than any other bird. Each year, it sets off from the Arctic Circle on its journey to the Antarctic, and then flies all the way back—a journey of about 18,600 miles (30,000 km).

The beak turns orange in spring and gray in winter.

Sea parrots

Colorful beaks give puffins the nickname "parrots of the sea." Large beaks are useful for grabbing lots of sand eels!

Star divers

Gannets have pointed wings, long beaks, and strong skulls. This lets them hit the water like a torpedo in pursuit of fishy prey. These seabirds can dive into water at speeds of up to 62 mph (100 kph).

Great gliders

Albatrosses fly for weeks at a time. With wings outstretched, they glide through the air. They are carried by the wind and hardly need to bother to flap!

The big scoop

Pelicans fly or swim in search of a fishy meal. When they spot fish, they dive down after them. They have stretchy throats for scooping up lots of fish in one gulp.

Fast facts

Seabirds have special features for life in water, such as webbed feet for swimming.

Water slides off their oily feathers so that they stay dry.

Gannets can dive to depths of 50 ft (15 m), while guillemots can dive 590 ft (180 m) under the water.

Mackerel migration
Fish such as mackerel (right) migrate in large schools (groups) every year to breed in shallow waters, or in search of food. They then swim back to the open waters where they started.

Broad flippers help turtles to "row" themselves forward.

Mackerel schools can be more than 5.5 miles (9 km) long.

Turtles probably find their way using Earth's magnetic field.

Going back home
Female green turtles travel to the place where they were born to lay their eggs, then swim back again across the open ocean.

Ocean travelers

Many sea creatures make amazing journeys, crisscrossing the oceans. They travel to find breeding grounds, food, or safety. This is called migration.

Lobster line-up
To escape storms, spiny lobsters walk along the seabed to deeper, calmer waters. They march head to tail. This makes it hard for predators to pick one out.

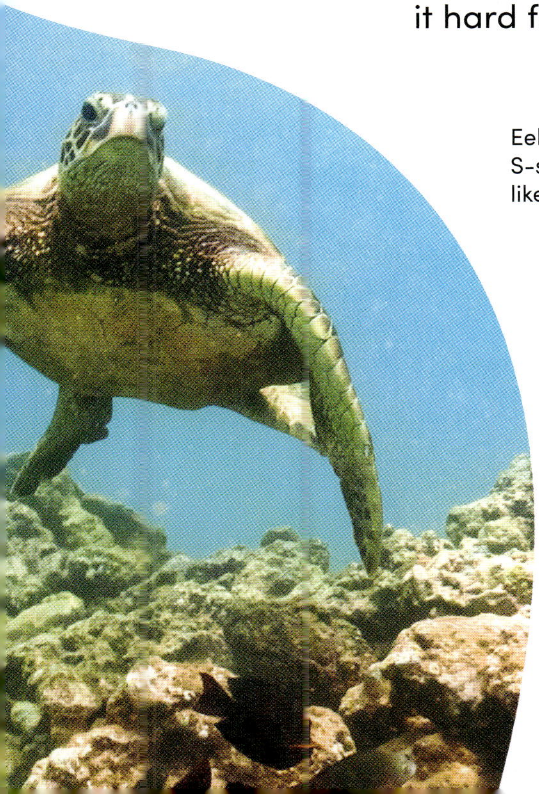

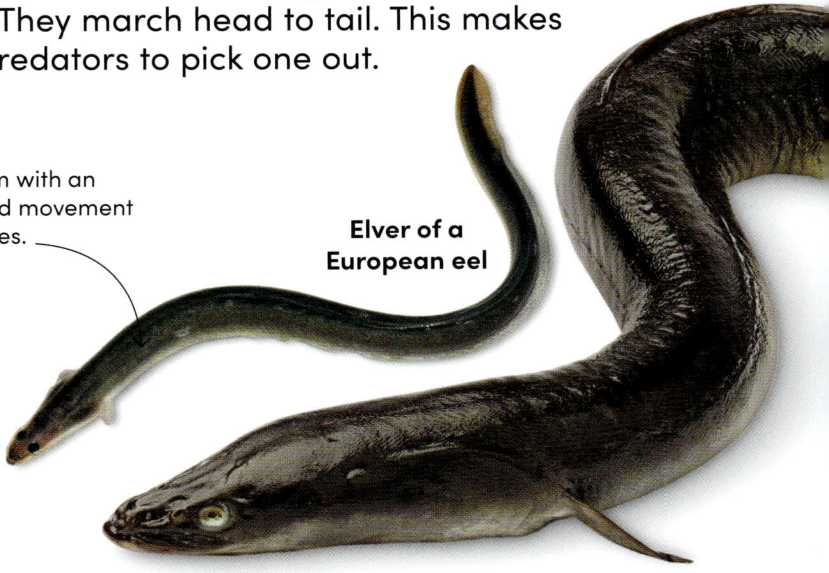

Eels swim with an S-shaped movement like snakes.

Elver of a European eel

Eels at sea
Eels travel from lakes and rivers to breed at sea. The young eels (elvers) then return to fresh water.

Octopuses and squid

These are fast underwater hunters that swim at high speed by squirting jets of water from their bag-like bodies. Octopuses and squid have long arms for seizing prey.

Shimmering squid

Many squid can produce their own light. Humboldt squid use lights to signal to each other as they hunt together in packs.

An octopus has a simple brain inside each arm.

Sweet dreams

Scientists have seen that an octopus sometimes changes the color of its skin when asleep. This could be the octopus having a dream!

Studded with suckers

Octopuses feel and taste with their eight arms. Each arm has rows of suckers that help them grip prey.

The flexible suckers can taste the things that they touch.

OCTOPUS OR SQUID?

Octopuses have eight arms, with suckers all the way along. Squid have eight arms with suckers that can have hooks on them, as well as two longer tentacles.

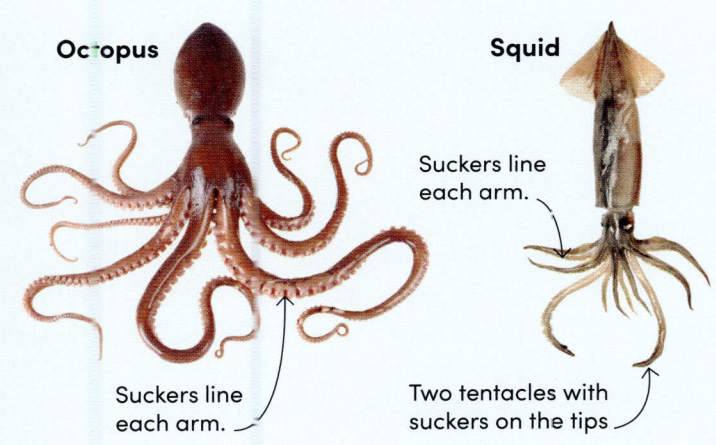

Octopus

Suckers line each arm.

Squid

Suckers line each arm.

Two tentacles with suckers on the tips

Ink attack!

To escape predators, octopuses and squid can play a clever trick. They squirt out a cloud of ink. While hidden in murky water, they make a getaway.

Living together

Different sea creatures may live together in a variety of fascinating ways. Often, the arrangement suits both creatures, but sometimes only one benefits.

Food for free

Remora fish attach themselves to larger fish, such as sharks. They eat fragments of food that drop from their host's mouth.

Remora fish

Brightly colored clown fish cannot hide easily.

Perfect partnership

Clown fish escape danger by darting into sea anemones. A coat of slime protects the fish from their stinging tentacles, and predators dare not follow.

Sea anemones have venomous tentacles.

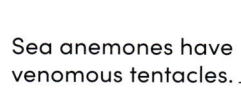

A bluestreak cleaner wrasse cleans the teeth of a coral grouper.

Cleaning service

Fish called cleaner wrasse set up cleaning stations in coral reefs. They eat parasites stuck to larger fish. Their customers have to wait in line!

Boxing gloves

Boxer crabs carry anemones and wave their stinging tentacles at predators. Anemones eat pieces of food the crabs drop.

Tangs have sharp teeth for nibbling algae.

Spring cleaning

Surgeonfish, such as tangs, sometimes nibble algae growing on turtles' shells. Turtles are glad to be cleaned up!

29

Down in the depths

No light reaches as far down as the ocean's deepest trenches. Here, animals live in freezing cold and total darkness. They have smart ways to survive on little food.

Daggerlike teeth line the fangtooth's huge jaws.

Underwater ogre

The gruesome looks of the fangtooth explain its other name, "ogre fish." When a fish or shrimp swims past, the fangtooth sucks it into its gigantic mouth.

Lying in wait

To save energy, tripod fish sit perched on the deep seabed on three long fins. They wait for food to come within reach.

Fishy fisherman

Anglerfish have a long fishing-rod fin with a light at the end. Small fish think that this is food. Lured toward it, they swim into the anglerfish's open jaws.

The light is produced by the bacteria living inside the rod.

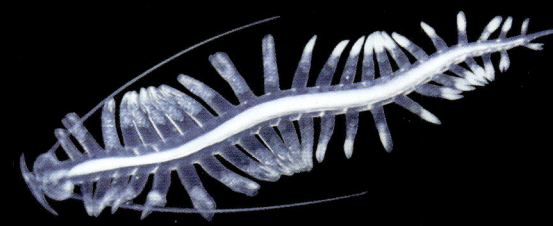

Transparent worms

Gossamer worms have delicate, see-through bodies, which hides them from predators.

 HIDE AND SEEK

Lantern fish (below) live in the twilight zone of the ocean, which gets very little sunlight. The fish can adjust the light it produces to match the low light in the water around it. Predators may struggle to spot it!

Fearsome hunter

The viperfish swims with its jaws open. It catches fish with its extra-long, sharp teeth.

The teeth form a cage that wriggling prey can't escape.

31

Life on the seabed

Lots of animals live underwater on the shallow seabed. These colorful creatures often look like plants, but they are really animals.

👁 **STARRING ROLE**

Brittle stars have brittle, easily broken arms. This does not matter because they can grow new ones! Like sea stars, brittle stars do not have a brain.

Seabed chimneys

Sponges come in strange shapes and many colors. They eat by capturing plankton as they pump water through their spongy bodies.

Colorful character

The vivid colors of sea slugs warn predators that they are poisonous and taste awful. This sea slug is called a "Spanish shawl" because it appears to have an orange fringe.

Fast facts

Sea stars, brittle stars, and sea cucumbers are seabed animals called echinoderms, which means "spiny skin."

Sea slugs eat anemones, corals, jellyfish, and sometimes even other sea slugs!

Some sea slugs steal the stings of the animals they eat, and use the stings to defend themselves.

This common sun star has 13 arms.

Spines cover the body and arms of this Bloody Henry starfish.

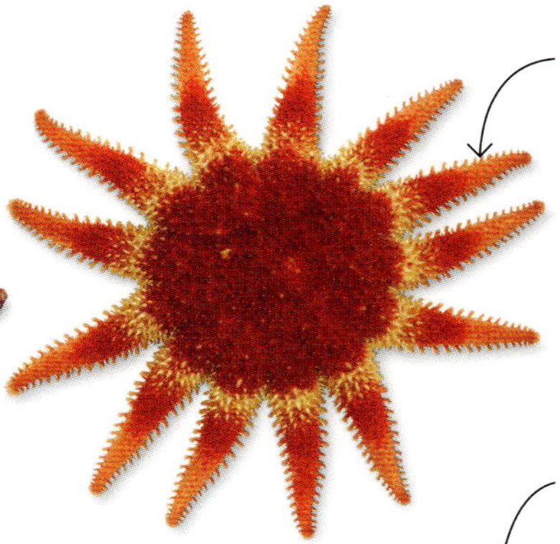

Sponges attach themselves to the seabed.

Some sponges can grow as tall as a 6 ft (1.8 m) human.

Hungry sea stars

Sea stars eat mussels and clams, using the suckers on their arms to pull the shells apart. Then they push their stomachs into the gap and eat up their prey.

Tentacles can be pulled back inside the body.

Row of feet

In the slow lane

Sea cucumbers crawl along the seabed at a snail's pace. They suck in food that sticks to their slimy tentacles.

Life in a coral reef

Corals are built by animals called polyps, which look like tiny flowers inside chalky, cup-shaped shelters. Reefs spread as new polyps grow on top of old ones. Many colorful animals hide in the reef.

House-hunting hermits

Hermit crabs often make their homes inside the empty shells of other animals. They may also move into small caves in the coral reef.

Fast facts

Tiny algae living inside the corals help them stay colorful.

Coral reefs grow in tropical oceans where the sea temperature is never below 68°F (20°C).

Australia's Great Barrier Reef is so large that it can be seen from space.

Slippery as an eel

Moray eels have slimy, snakelike bodies. They slither into caves and crevices to hide during the day, coming out at night to hunt for food.

Pacific sea horse

A twist of the tail

To anchor themselves, sea horses twist their tails around corals. If an enemy appears, they change color to match their surroundings.

A WORLD OF CORALS

Rose coral
This coral is like a rose. It can be huge—up to 6.5 ft (2 m) wide.

Daisy coral
These tough corals have polyps that look like daisy flowers.

Brain coral
Wiggly lines cover this coral, which looks like a human brain!

Sea fans
Some corals grow like trees or bushes, or flat like a lacy fan.

Underwater butterflies

With their slim bodies, butterfly fish can dart in and out of gaps in the coral. Butterfly fish eat plankton and some snack on coral polyps.

Butterfly fish

Coral reefs look like underwater gardens.

Icy waters

The waters of the northern and southern polar regions are partly frozen. Many animals that live here have a thick layer of fat, called blubber, to keep warm.

Coming up for air

Like all mammals, seals breathe air. They gnaw at sea ice with their sharp teeth to keep air holes open for breathing.

Fast facts

Harp seal pups drink their mothers' milk for about two weeks, then find their own food.

Growing up to 10 ft (3 m) high, a polar bear is nearly twice as tall as a human being.

Polar bears build snow dens to shelter their cubs.

The tusks (long front teeth) of a walrus can grow up to 3.3 ft (1 m) long.

Noisy walruses

Walruses live in large groups around the North Pole. These noisy animals bark, growl, and whistle to each other.

Swimming under ice

Polar bears hunt prey in icy Arctic seas. Their slightly webbed toes help them to swim. They paddle with their front legs and steer with their hind ones.

Polar bears have black skin under their white fur.

👁 USEFUL FUR

Harp seal pups are born with white fur that camouflages them on the ice. This is useful because they often wait alone for their mothers to return from feeding. Unlike adult harp seals, pups don't have blubber at birth, so the white fur keeps them warm.

In the water

Penguins are speedy swimmers, but they have little defense against predators. In water, their dark backs and light-colored bellies act as camouflage. This is known as countershading.

Flipper-like wing rows penguin along under water.

Fast facts

Emperor penguins can dive down to more than 1,640 ft (500 m), taking them into the midnight zone.

The emperor penguin is the largest penguin of all.

Many penguins live in the coldest, windiest place in the world—the southernmost, icy continent of Antarctica.

Birds of a feather

Emperor penguin chicks have gray, fluffy feathers. Later, they grow black and white feathers like their parents.

Nursery on the ice

Emperor penguin chicks and adults huddle together in groups of up to 5,000 birds. It is much warmer inside the huddle than outside it.

Penguin party

Penguins are birds, but they cannot fly. Most penguins live in Earth's southern waters. Shiny, waterproof feathers prevent their skin from getting wet and fluffy feathers trap a warm layer of air underneath.

A penguin has a large head and a short neck.

DARING DIVERS

Adélie penguins are the most common Antarctic penguins. They dive into the icy water to hunt for fish and squid. Swimming at speed, they can launch themselves from the water on to the shore.

Perfect parent

After laying eggs, female emperor penguins return to the sea. In the icy winter, the males keep the eggs warm on their feet. When the chicks hatch, their mothers return to feed them.

Kingdom of kelp

Hidden under the waves are large forests of seaweed called kelp. These towering algae are like high-rise apartments, providing homes and food for sea creatures at every level.

Leaflike fronds stay upright and float near the surface.

Super snacks

Kelp attracts schools of small fish that can make a good meal for harbor seals. After eating, the seals relax in the canopy of kelp near the water's surface.

Hanging out

Sea otters lie in hammocks of kelp. Their waterproof fur is so thick that their skin never gets wet! They use their bellies as tables for laying out meals.

Blue fish

In the kelp forests of Australia live large fish called blue gropers. They can live for 70 years. Snorkelers often get to know these friendly fish and give them names.

Sea lions

These mammals get their name from roaring like lions. In the kelp, they eat clams, crabs, fish, and lobsters. They are fast swimmers, with winglike front flippers.

Kelp can grow 20 in (50 cm) a day.

👁 FOREST FLAME

Flame-colored garibaldis have small territories in the kelp. If a neighbor gets too close, the garibaldis confront each other face to face. They wave their tails furiously.

Exploring underwater

So much of Earth's oceans is yet to be explored! To survive underwater, human divers need special clothing and equipment. When descending to great depths, they travel in underwater vehicles called submersibles.

Marine scientists go on scuba dives to observe ocean life.

Scuba diving

Scuba (Self-Contained, Underwater Breathing Apparatus) allows divers to breathe from tanks of air strapped to their backs.

Robotic explorers

Deep-sea machines with no people inside are called remotely operated vehicles, or ROVs. Scientists use them to study the deep sea with cameras and robotic arms controlled from a ship at the surface.

This robotic machine is exploring the remains of a boat that sank in 1844.

Diving vehicles

Submersibles may help to explore the deep ocean safely. The submersible *Nautile* (right) can dive to nearly 19,700 ft (6,000 m). Here, it is launched in the Atlantic Ocean to explore the wreck of the passenger ship *Titanic* (below).

Titanic disaster

Shipwrecks come to rest on the seabed. In 1912, the ship *Titanic* hit an iceberg and sank on its first-ever voyage. The submersible *Nautile* took nearly two hours to reach it, to explore this famous shipwreck.

Pollution problems

The oceans are under threat from pollution caused by people. Our day-to-day activities are making the world's waters an unhealthy home for all kinds of marine life.

Plastic everywhere

Plastic waste floats down rivers into the oceans. It creates huge trash dumps in the water and endangers marine life.

Polar bears use sea ice to travel and hunt in their Arctic home.

Warmer world

Burning fossil fuels, such as oil and gas, makes the planet hotter. This melts sea ice, making life difficult for animals such as polar bears, and sea levels rise, endangering coastal settlements.

Bleached coral

Fast facts

It may take a coral reef up to 10 years to recover after bleaching.

Oil tankers are big ships that sometimes spill oil into the oceans and poison marine life.

The Great Pacific Garbage Patch is a huge heap of plastic floating on the Pacific Ocean. It is three times the size of France.

Losing color

Coral reefs provide a home to millions of different sea creatures. But as the oceans warm up, the coral turns white and dies out. This process is called coral bleaching.

SAVE OUR SEAS

There are solutions to all these problems. Reducing and recycling plastic creates less waste. The sun and wind are alternative energy sources to fossil fuels. To save dying coral reefs, marine biologists grow coral in underwater nurseries before planting them back in the reefs or add heat-resistant algae to these reefs (shown on the right).

Floating plastic can trap or poison marine creatures.

Huahine Island reef, French Polynesia

Warmer waters make the algae inside the corals leave, turning them white.

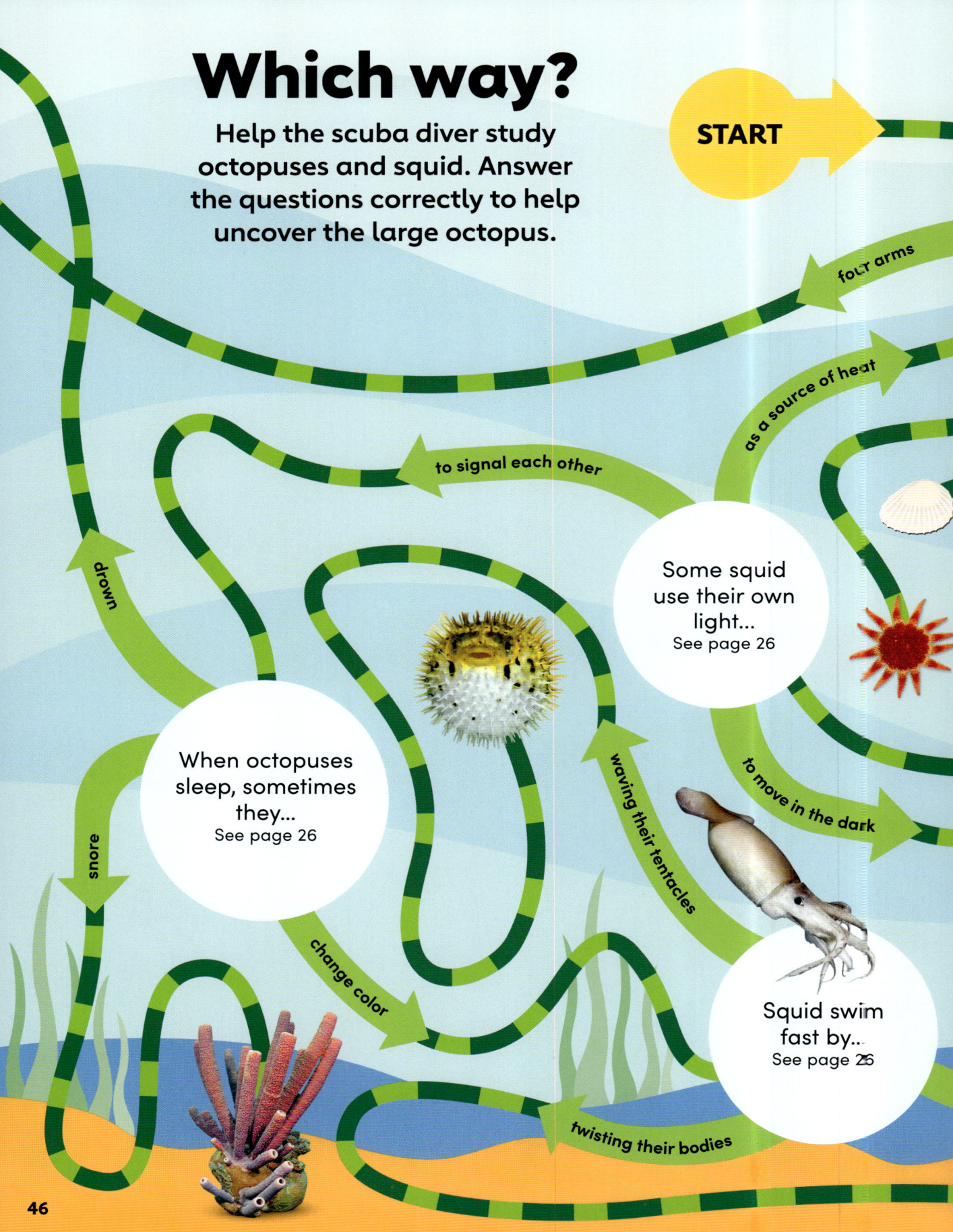

Which way?

Help the scuba diver study octopuses and squid. Answer the questions correctly to help uncover the large octopus.

START

four arms

as a source of heat

to signal each other

drown

Some squid use their own light...
See page 26

When octopuses sleep, sometimes they...
See page 26

snore

waving their tentacles

to move in the dark

change color

Squid swim fast by...
See page 26

twisting their bodies

Octopuses feel and taste with their...
See page 27

six arms

hide behind other creatures

When in danger, octopuses...
See page 27

eight arms

inflate their bodies

grip prey

squirt a cloud of ink

The suckers on the tentacles help octopuses to...
See page 27

swim around

fight predators

squirting jets of water

FINISH

Who am I?

Take a look at these close-ups of animals in the book, and see if you can identify them. The clues should help you!

3
- I have a striped body.
- My poisonous spines will pierce any predator that bites me.

1
- I live in a social group called a pod.
- I am a toothed whale.

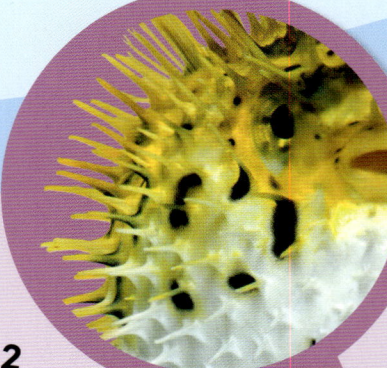

2
- I have spines.
- When threatened, I gulp down water and swell up like a balloon.

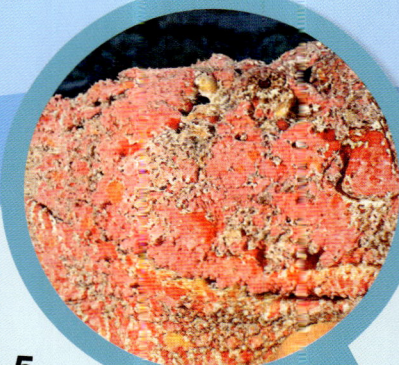

5
- I change color to look like part of the seabed.
- I have spines on my back for protection.

4
- To escape danger, I dart into anemones.
- I am a brightly colored fish.

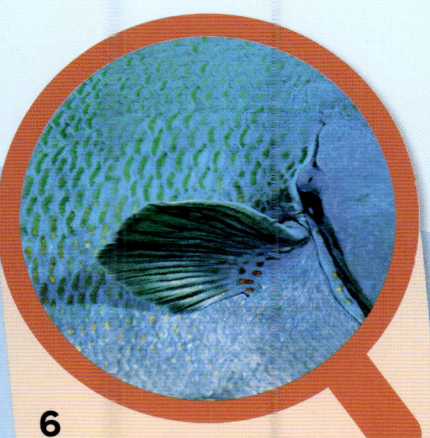

7

🐟 I am more than 95 percent water.

🐟 I have no brain, bones, heart, or eyes.

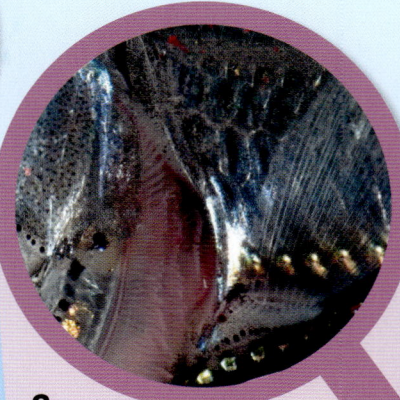

6

🐟 I am a friendly fish living in a kelp forest.

🐟 I am a lovely, bright blue color.

8

🐟 I have long, sharp teeth.

🐟 I live in the dark, deep ocean.

10

🐟 I have a muscly body and many arms.

🐟 I have a brain in each arm.

9

🐟 I live in a shell abandoned by other animals.

🐟 I may also live in a small cave on a coral reef.

11

🐟 Tiny animals called polyps build me.

🐟 I look like a human brain.

Answers: 1.Orca 2.Porcupine fish 3.Lionfish 4.Clown fish 5.Stonefish 6.Blue groper 7.Jellyfish 8.Viperfish 9.Hermit crab 10.Octopus 11.Brain coral

Facts match

Revisit the underwater world. Read the clues below and see if you can find the correct answers among the pictures.

1. I crawl along the seabed at a snail's pace.

Kelp

Rose coral

Sea star

Manatee

Leopard shark

Cleaner wrasse

Sea otter

2. I provide food and shelter for all sorts of sea creatures.

3. I have eyes at each end of my unusually wide head.

4. I get my name from my spotted skin. Clams are my favorite food.

5. I eat parasites stuck to larger fish such as coral groupers.

6. We capture plankton and feed on it by pumping water through our bodies.

7. I look like a flower. I can grow up to 6.5 ft (2 m) wide.

8. I'm a plant-eating sea mammal, like the dugong. I eat sea grass.

9. I pull mussels and clams apart by using the suckers on my arms.

Leafy sea dragon

Sponges

Hammerhead shark

Butterfly fish

Sea cucumber

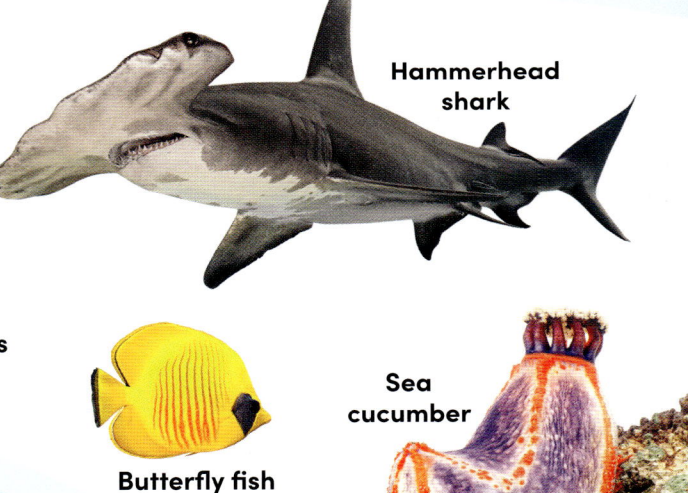

10. I live in shallow, seaweedy waters and look like seaweed.

11. My waterproof fur is so thick that my skin never gets wet.

12. With my slim body, I can dart in and out of gaps in the coral.

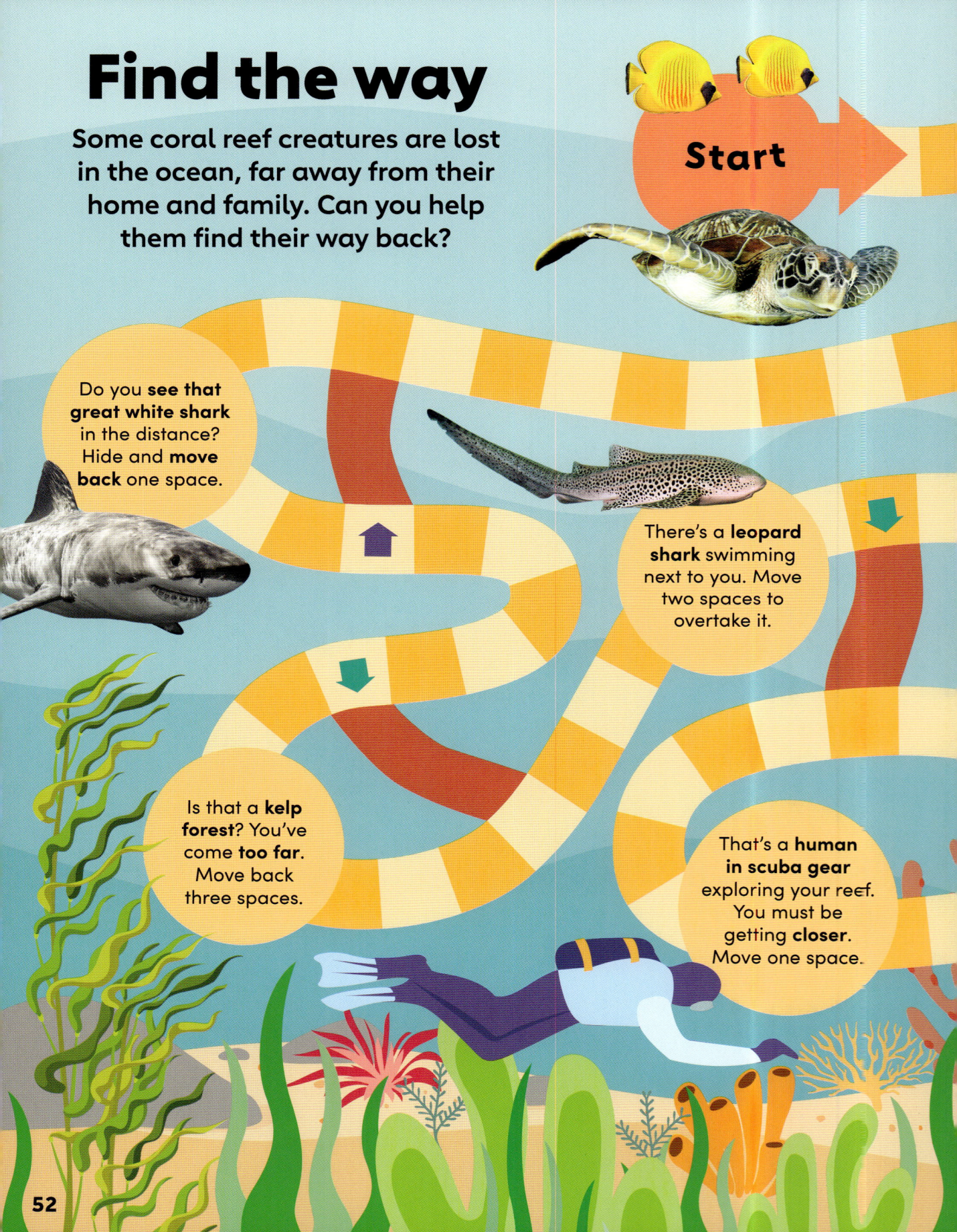

Find the way

Some coral reef creatures are lost in the ocean, far away from their home and family. Can you help them find their way back?

Start

Do you **see that great white shark** in the distance? Hide and **move back** one space.

There's a **leopard shark** swimming next to you. Move two spaces to overtake it.

Is that a **kelp forest**? You've come **too far**. Move back three spaces.

That's a **human in scuba gear** exploring your reef. You must be getting **closer**. Move one space.

How to play

This is a game for up to four players.

Move down!

Move up!

You will need a die and counters for each player. You could use counters from other board games you might have, or you could make your own counters with colored paper—one color for each player.

Each player takes turns to throw the dice, and begins from the START box. Follow the squares with each roll of the dice. If you land on an instruction, make sure you do as it says. Good luck!

Is that a **lionfish flaring its fins**? Skirt around it **carefully**. Move one space.

You've run into a **cluster of jellyfish**. Try to avoid their sting and quickly move one space

Avoid getting stung by that anemone and **move** two spaces.

Wait! There's **an orca, and it can eat you**! Hide, hide, hide, and miss a turn!

You're in your **coral reef**! Move three spaces and join your family!

You're home!

Glossary

Algae Simple plantlike organisms that live in or near water.

Animal A living thing that eats and reacts to its surroundings. Most animals can move around too.

Antarctic The vast continent covered in ice in Earth's south.

Arctic The mass of ice-covered ocean and surrounding land at the very north of our planet.

Baleen The brushlike fringe in the mouths of some whales, used to strain tiny food out of seawater.

Blubber A thick layer of fat that keeps polar animals and whales warm in cold waters.

Breeding The process by which fully grown animals produce babies.

Camouflage The colors or patterns on an animal's skin or fur that helps them blend in where they live to stay safe or hunt more easily.

Canopy The very top of the trees in a forest, including kelp forests in the ocean.

Carnivore An animal that eats only meat.

Coast The stretch of land along the ocean.

Continental shelf The shallow part of the ocean floor that meets with the land.

Countershading The protective effect of having a darker back and a pale tummy in water. From above, a dark back blends in with the darkness of the deep sea. From below, a pale tummy merges with the light from the sky above.

Crustacean A type of animal with a hard shell and jointed legs that lives mostly in water. Crabs and lobsters are crustaceans.

Echinoderms A type of animal with spiny skin and tubelike feet, but no backbone, brain, or heart. Sea cucumbers are echinoderms.

Equator An imaginary line around the center of Earth that is an equal distance from the North and South poles.

Gills The parts of a fish that allow them to breathe underwater.

Invertebrate An animal that does not have a backbone.

Kelp A type of giant seaweed that grows in huge clumps in the ocean.

Luminous Something that shines or gives off light. Some fish in the deep ocean produce their own luminous effect.

Mammal A warm-blooded animal with a backbone that is covered in hair or fur, and breathes oxygen from the air. Female mammals produce milk to feed their young.

Mollusk An animal with a soft body and no backbone that is sometimes covered by a protective shell.

Oceanography The name for the study of the oceans and seas.

Oxygen A colorless gas that almost all living things need to breathe or take in to stay alive.

Parasite An animal that lives on or inside another animal in order to feed off it.

Plankton Tiny creatures that live in water in big numbers and provide food for larger animals.

Polar region The very cold areas near the North Pole or the South Pole of Earth.

Predator An animal that hunts other living animals for food.

Prey An animal that is hunted by other animals for food.

Scales The tiny protective plates that cover fish and reptiles.

Sea A large area of saltwater that is smaller than an ocean, often partly or completely surrounded by land.

Seashore The strip of sand or rock that borders the sea.

Species A group of animals or plants with shared features that can breed and produce babies together.

Streamlined A smooth shape that helps an animal move easily through the water.

Submersible A boat or machine that can travel underwater to explore the deep ocean.

Tentacles Long, moving feelers that some animals have on their heads for feeling and feeding. Jellyfish and squid have tentacles.

Territory The area where an animal lives and defends against other animals moving in.

Vertebrate An animal that has a backbone.

Animal alphabet

Every animal pictured in this book is listed here in alphabetical order. Use the page numbers to find them.

Albatross 23
A seabird with the largest wingspan of any bird that soars over the ocean.

Anglerfish 31
A fish that dangles a light from its head to attract prey in the deep, dark ocean.

Arctic tern 22
A seabird that makes the longest journey of any bird, flying from its breeding grounds in the Arctic to its feeding grounds in the Antarctic.

Blue groper 40
A large fish that lives in warm waters off the coastline of Australia.

Brittle star 32
A star-shaped, round-bodied echinoderm with five long, thin arms that wriggle around like snakes.

Butterfly fish 35
A brightly colored fish that uses it bristle-like teeth to feed on coral in reefs around the world.

Cleaner wrasse 28
A small fish that feeds on parasites stuck to larger fish and cleans their bodies in the process.

Clown fish 24
A colorful fish that lives in among sea anemones on coral reefs, so it is protected against predators.

Coral 35
Animals that live in colonies of hundreds of tiny bodies called polyps. Some build huge reefs.

Crab 29
This tough-shelled, ten-legged crustacean moves sideways along the floor of coral reefs or rocky shores.

Dolphin 19
A smooth, streamlined mammal that swims easily through the waters of the sunlight zone.

Dugong 20–21
A large mammal that grazes on seagrass in the warm waters of the Pacific and Indian oceans.

Eel 25, 34
These long, snakelike fish hide in among the coral reefs by day and come out at night to hunt for fish and crustaceans.

Fangtooth 30
A fish with a huge mouth and sharp teeth to bite into passing prey in the deep ocean.

Garibaldi fish 30
A bright orange fish that feeds in the kelp forests off the west coast of the United States.

Gannet 23
A large seabird that dives down to feed on fish in the Atlantic Ocean.

Gossamer worm 31
A segmented, see-through worm that swims in the deep sea where it can produce its own light.

Jellyfish 12
A soft-bodied marine creature with trailing tentacles to sting prey in coastal waters around the world.

Lantern fish 31
A small fish that creates a glow in the dark depths of the ocean.

Leafy sea dragon 10
A fish with a horse-shaped head, tube-shaped mouth, and frilly body that lives in the kelp forests of Australia.

Lionfish 10
A spiny fish equipped with poisonous spines to defend itself in the coral reefs.

Mackerel 24
A fast fish that travels in large groups to hunt down small marine life in the Pacific, Atlantic, and Indian oceans.

Manatee 20–21
A big, bulky mammal, known as a sea cow, because it munches on seagrass in warm, shallow waters.

Manta ray 11
A large, flat fish with fins like wings that flaps through the water with its mouth open to feed in the tropical waters all around the world.

Octopus 26
An eight-armed mollusk with blue blood and three hearts that lives in oceans throughout the world.

Pelican 23
A big seabird that hunts along coastlines or riverbanks by dipping its bill under the surface to catch fish.

Penguin 38–39
A stocky seabird that cannot fly, but can swim at high speed in the chilly waters of Antarctica.

Plankton 7
The tiniest marine life that builds up into giant shoals, providing a feast for fish in the Pacific and Atlantic oceans.

Porcupine fish 11
A spiky fish that blows itself up like a balloon to look bigger and scare off predators in the coral reefs.

Portuguese man-of-war 13
A close relative of jellyfish, this marine creature floats through tropical waters, using its trailing tentacles to deliver a powerful sting to prey.

Polar bear 37
An enormous white bear that hunts for seals in the Arctic waters.

Puffin 22
A small seabird that eats fish and lives in large numbers along rocky coastlines of the Pacific and Atlantic oceans.

Remora 25
A type of fish that attaches itself to bigger fish, including sharks and manta rays, to feed on their parasites and food scraps in tropical waters.

Saupe 9
A small, yellow-striped fish that swims in large shoals for safety in the warm waters where it lives.

Sea anemone 28
A close relative of jellyfish, this soft-bodied creature has stinging tentacles to protect itself against predators in the coral reefs.

Sea cucumber 33
A cucumber-shaped echinoderm that lives on the seabed in shallow and deep waters around the world.

Sea lion 41
A large mammal covered in a thick layer of blubber to keep warm in the chilly waters of the Pacific Ocean.

Sea otter 40
A small mammal with incredibly thick, waterproof fur to withstand the cold temperatures of the north Pacific Ocean.

Sea slug 33
A colorful mollusk without a shell that usually slides along the seabed.

Sea star 33
A star-shaped echinoderm that typically has five arms, but can have many more, and exists in all the world's oceans.

Sea turtle 24
A large marine reptile with a protective shell that uses its streamlined flippers to power through most oceans except the polar regions.

Sea horse 34
A small fish with a horse-shaped head that floats upright in the Pacific, Indian, and Atlantic oceans, using its tubelike mouth to suck up food.

Seal 37, 40
A smooth, streamlined mammal with plenty of blubber to keep out the chill of the Arctic and Atlantic oceans.

Shark 8, 9, 14–15
A typically large fish with a tough body that hunts in all the world's oceans, but prefers warmer waters.

Shearwater 6
A seabird that hunts fish by skimming low over the surface of the Pacific, Indian, and Atlantic oceans.

Spiny lobster 25
A large crustacean with a spiny shell that feeds on small marine life in tropical waters.

Sponge 32
A simple marine animal with no heart or backbone that stays in one place on the coral reefs or shallow seabed as an adult.

Squid 26
A close relative of the octopus, this fast-moving mollusk has eight arms and two tentacles to hold prey. It lives in all the world's oceans.

Stonefish 10
A type of venomous fish that lies low on the seabed in the Pacific and Indian oceans using its spines to defend themselves from attackers.

Tang 29
A brightly colored fish that eats algae in coral reefs.

Tripod fish 30
An unusual fish with three long, leglike fins it uses to perch on the seabed in the deep ocean.

Viperfish 31
A small fish with deadly jaws and sharp teeth ready to sink into prey in the deep sea.

Walrus 36
A massive mammal with thick blubber and long, strong tusks to survive along the remote Arctic coastline.

Whale 6, 15, 16–17
A truly enormous sea mammal that breathes through a blowhole on top of its head and lives everywhere in the open ocean.